THE MOURNERS' BENCH
And Other Stations of Weeping
and Joy

by

BILLYE OKERA

ISBN: 1-938373-10-3

ISBN 13: 978-1-938373-10-7

© 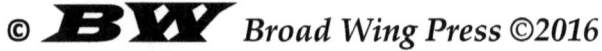 Broad Wing Press ©2016

Lanham, MD

"You know my coins are counterfeit
But you accept them anyway
My impudence and my pretending"

Rumi
"I Have Five Things to Say"

CONTENTS

PROLOGUE 1
    Poem 2

THE BISHOPRIC
And Other Multi-Syllabic Epiphanies................................3

FOR MICHAEL, MY BROTHA..11
    Fireside Dreams.. 12
    Pale Horse Riding 13
    Liquid..14
    The Brotha with the Fine Taste 15
    Write a Poem About It...17
    For Michael My Brotha 18
    What is Your Death to Me 20
    Sicklerville 21
    For Michael. . .Again.. 22
    Six Months After 23

BETWIXT and BETWEEN 25
    Silk Screen 26
    You Who Stayed...27
    As the Leaf 28
    Damascus 29
    Still Running 31
    Face to Face 32
    Betwixt and Between 35
    If it Weren't for Death..37

Positive Self-Talk 39
God Must Know 40
God Calls 42
Thoughts After a Night of Depression 43
Good Time Music 46
The One Who Danced 47
Conversation with God 48
Jubilee 53
He Comes 55
Prophecy 58

THE MOURNERS' BENCH 61
Spotsylvania Legacy 62
Senseless Fire 63
The Woe of a Child 64
Fault 66
Harriet Tubman 67
What the Anger Feels like 69
Jesse's Brown 70
The Mourners' Bench 72
Purge 73

BLURRED PHOTOGRAPHS 75
Motown Melodies 76
Blurred Photographs 78
Solid 82
Father Memory 83
...Who Cannot Speak of Our Fathers 84
Father 85
I Do Not Hug My Sister 86

This Winter's Day 87
Anointing 88
She Lay Dying 89
About Washington 90
In Georgetown 94
Rehoboth 95
When I Die 98

A WOMAN'S PARANOIA 102
I Am 103
Seein' Red 104
The Spring of that First Love 105
Paradigm 108
Rockin' and Hummin' 110
Her Face in Glass 112
Lonely 113
Blue Prints 115
A Woman's Paranoia 116
One Who Loves Me 118
It's Time 120
Rise 121
Understanding 122
Strong Black Woman 124
Vanity 125
Virtuous Woman 126
Will You Ever Know My Soul? 128
Worthy 129
Soap-Opera Divas 130
Renewal 131
Cacklin with Cicada 132

    By All Means 135
    I Have Crawled into that Space 137

EPILOGUE 140
    I Am a Woman Growing Older 141

ABOUT THE AUTHOR 145

PROLOGUE

POEM

If the poem is not
Then I am not. If word had not joined
This pull back from the brink
Then what you think you see
Is travesty - as it is said
Illusion - imagery called
From desire. So if this be
I will put word to page to ply song
From the night-winds
Weeping - conjure mountain magnificence
Page praying your smile while this word I write
Whittles the world with wonder.
Pulling asunder
What we know of death
Word will whisper a new order
From the old. It will alter sacrifice
Of blood to celebration and our dancing days
We will not repent of
Nor will shadow seep
Into curlicues and twist blistering the sands
Of our joy. If it is my word
And this time it is
I claim it mine!
With rhyme and root forgiving
Past dalliance in pain. Pen and parchment
Glowing with the glory of the earth
My birth no longer limp
From absent testament.

THE BISHOPRIC
& Other Multi-Syllabic Epiphanies

I

Preacha preachin'
Power perfect prose. Pleadin' passions
Prays people pay.

II

Ma Bessie snatchin' hats
With dangles
Entangled in madness.

III

Bishop Dunn cinched tightly
At the waist. 0 for a taste
Of that man.

IV

Convocation in August
Brotha couldn't remember
My name.

V

Preacha's kid say
He didn't do what He did
I know He did it. Get it.

VI

Sistah Strobel struts
The sanctuary isle in style
Hoe-down, chile.

VII
Bishop breakin' bread
Bitchin bout Betty's baby
His, maybe?

    VIII
Bishop needin' his chow
Sistah slavin' on the fiery clay
Bring the gold tray,
Now!

    IX
Pastor practice laying on hands
Cause he be the man
Lay down, honey.

    X
Pastor needin' space
To place his books,
Church gonna buy him a house.

    XI
Pastor wanting a new suit
And shirt and socks
And tock for tellin time
Yours 'ill do fine

    XII
Talk to the priest- tell him
Cease genuflecting in the isles
God's eyes are closed.

XIII
Rain raging upon the roof
Street people under bridge
Safe at home.

XIV

The silence on my lips
The silence of your heart
The valley of death.

XV
The child is not crying
The child is not laughing
Bethlehem's asleep.

XVI
The stone is rolled away
The grave clothes tossed aside
Not even a ghost.

XVII
Roses growing hearty
Using new fertilizer
Mother died last night.

XVIII
Now that
The holocaust is over
When does the party start.

XVIV
The Spirit motions to the heart
Of malevolent men
Slamming doors.

XX
When rain comes again, God
Will I know the memory
Of this sunshine?

XXI
Green greatness garners
Total supplication
My desert is spreading.

XXII
Prozac and Praxil
Transcendental Meditation
Demons still dance.

XIII
Talk to the doctor - tell him
That with pluck 'n pinch 'n tuck
Time will be made a fool of.

XXIV
Count to ten
In a minute the rage will stop
And you can go on lying.

XXV
Close the shutters
You are no longer young
And walkers have stopped watching
Your nakedness.

XXVI
I can guess what you are thinking
I can see it on your face
When was the last time
We saw God crying?

XXVII
Hobgoblins gather
At the ghosting gate
I am late for eternity.

XXVIII
My mama
Taught me many things
You doubt why I am a fool?

XXVIV
Mama's been dead twelve years
Her grave unmarked
In stark recognition.

XXX
Nothing my father said
Is recorded for my posterity
I know why some are stillborn.

XXXI
My father hung himself on alcohol
Jesus hung himself on a cross
... the greater loss?

XXXII
Of all the folk I know
In tomb and vault and grave
Not a word of caution.

XXXIII
Clear up this place.
It's a disgrace the things left
For scavengers and would be lovers.

XXXIV
If the cost of love
Is that I sell you my soul
The sale is cancelled.

XXXV
Possession is nine-tenths law
Sir, you have some claim
To my sanity?

XXXVI
Ha! I've been battered
By better beast than you, Brotha
My shadow trips met

XXXVII
Stop asking for change
Left over from my dollar
I've just enough to ride the rails
To nowhere.

XXXVIII
Touch that again
And you will pay mightily
My soul is bold against intruders.

XXXVIV
Gather the crumbs
Left by lying lovers
Swallow the whole of them
And live.

XXXX
My sisters be preachas
I am a poet
Is anyone saved?

FOR MICHAEL, MY BROTHA

Given his complicity in his own death
What has Michael to do
With my nightmare?

FIRESIDE DREAMS

Fireside dreams have fallen by the way.
I once would say of life
I am the center of it all
And all is to my bidding -
That I will wake and death and time be stilled.
But, word is word
No magic has transpired from this reverie
Time still flows . . .
      Death still stalks   .
          Your still gone   .
Fireside dreams have fallen by the way.

PALE HORSE RIDING

Memories from yesterday into my room
A pale horse riding hi-ho silver dreams
Nightmare runners yelling "ho-boy"
Trampling through tracking truth
And taking soul-spoils to the victor.
I was bold boasting nothing of this thievery.
Mount me . . .
      Harness hope
             From the womb of this death
Waste not one moment galloping from this terror.

LIQUID

Wait! Morning's not for questions.
Let Prozac and caffeine glean giddiness
From games played yesterday.
Wait until I wake 'n pour gin & tonic
And demonic memory
Into my glass of liquid strength.

THE BROTHA WITH THE FINE TASTE

I just be needing something from you
Can't say baby I need
Lest you play that hiding game you do
When it ain't about yo needs but mine.
Been long needing them arms
You fold me in like rock
And that mind I grinds my spirit on.
You got a way of pulling scabs from closed places
Then moving on with blood flowing
And the pain oozing from yesterday.
You got a way of goin' low wid me
And forcing gut sounds from the pit
Of every gone lover.

I jes be calling my amens to yo. brotha
      With the fine taste
But the wasted eyes staring past my need.
I been wanting to give you things
Kneel before you like prayer
Sing my song, say my poem
Conjure my potion over you
In benediction for every heartless trespass
Like I was magic and my spell was solid.

But, you got an absent soul
And an absent heart
Only yo body don't know it.
I just be needing something
To hold on to

To bare me through yo midnight forages through me
Yo half remembered promises
Yo calm lies that wake dead places
Then lay me dead again.

WRITE A POEM ABOUT IT

(Michael told me this one month before he committed suicide: "This pain I cause you is worth your usual response")

You say whaaaaaaaatt, brothaaaaaa?
Write a poem about it like you usually do
Ask the muse for benediction
Pronounce it well worth wordy exaltations
Air it out.
Don't hide it under logs lying lone in dead wood
Away from soothsayers prophesying pleasant turns of phase
      Or event.
You say. . . itttttt. . . 'ill passssssss. Journal on it, baby
That's what you do.
From January first to December last
Alpha, omega, beginning, end - begin documenting days
Playing passioned scenes through to cruel endings.
Have the stage crew wipe the set of sweat
To lessen the chances of us falling.
Fall anyway 'n have a heave-ho out the door
Push to the side of the balcony out there
Where the neighbors haven't a clue to death creeping
Past blood stained post
      Surrender. Remove the mask   tack it to a tree
Tastefully offer it tea and Lorna Dunes
And pistachio nut ice cream and have it sit a while exposed.
Undress it. Naked lay it upon your altar
Raise you knife
Hoping some kind deity places ram in bush
      To stay the hand of sacrifice.

FOR MICHAEL MY BROTHA
(Who committed suicide July 19. 1997)

How can you - you who held me
Just those short days ago
Go into the earth spoiled and stiff
Unaware I stand at the end of a deep well . . . watching
With eyes too stunned to believe
And heart to hollow to feel?
Did you know some things of death I didn't?
Did it promise you some comfort
I have long since known it did not hold?
Did its laughter mock - tease you
Absent hope or vision for tomorrow?
Did it speak to you differently
Promise you a plush room with demitasse
And continental breakfast
Say of the accommodations nothing's spared
For those brave enough to come?
You Fool! Trouble is now gone - you can't come back.
I've seen the cramped box containing what remains!
But where have You gone?
Surely that bullet marked body
Naked on a white slab cannot be you.
Short of the pain you left
Short of revenge of the meanest kind
What has your death brought
But earth and worms
And funeral songs mocking the shroud
Yo' mama bought thinking to lay you calm
And easy into the night

Into the not knowing
Of one damning struggle believing he could not win
And buying all chances to himself?
How Arrogant. Your pain. Your loss.
Your discomfort. Your needs unmet

You selfish son-of-a-bitch!
You died lying to us all
And all of us tsk, tsk, tsking
And what-a-shaming - hanging our heads . . .
    Crying . . . for the things we did not do
To stop you.

WHAT IS YOUR DEATH TO ME?

What is your death to me?
Prozac days and vodka nights
Are hardly barometers of pain.
I believe God could crack the sky
And I - stoically upon your grave would stand
Without wink or wince. It's been one month since
Thirty twenty-four hour nightmares
Of you gone and not returning.
It is your face that I must see!
Polaroid and Kodak takes do little justice to the thought
Of your strong arms folded in crumbling coverlet of earth.
     I am not mad
I say a thing knowing the consequence is mine -
Did not God have better things to do
Than peel your life and laughter from me?
Couldn't He - in some other field
Have played capricious deity
And left us to our loving?
Was there no other fool fated for frolic
In the arms of death? I stand bereft of grief.
Serotonin re-uptake inhibitors forbid tears
And years from now - having never cried
That damnable tide will carry me away.

SICKLERVILLE

We were forever after Michael and me.
Michael came all the way from Sicklerville
With his dark
Thinking morning would break
And son-light wake us up.
He fell into place
What little grace, joy and kindness
Fell to madness
And, no coherent question ever asked again.
Coming home was such desolation.
Rich sunsets take mourning sky for granted
Oblivion's no victory
Not knowing the reason for the kill.
    Me? Still bewildered
By this travesty
    Why?

FOR MICHAEL...AGAIN

Give grief her voice
Not this stifled sanction of your going
Beyond my reach
Whys and what-ifs . . . sobered in Prozac memory -
But appropriate grief:
At the sound of the toll - soul should'a leapt
And begged pardon for its trek
     On complex lovin
This is a goin ill-advised my brotha/friend
Search heaven or hell . . . Then tell me
When can you walk this way . . .
Again?

SIX MONTHS AFTER
For Michael, My Brother (A Benediction)

God of my morning hour
Of thought racing about dreams finding their endings
And jazz tunes blowin
      Bendin about pillow worn from weary flesh
Startled from sleep - I'd-stretch -my arms - in-praise-
Had I not been so lost in the night
Dazed by hopeless longing and the memory
      Of haunted footpaths
Had I been able to sing a bit or dance
With the saints in sanctuary -
Ceasing the constant reverie to this pain
Adoring all that bore me to it
Had I walked the other-way from my own calamities
And having failed forgiven my own trespass
Were it not always about yesterday
And how far tomorrows be for one iced in the past
Had I not been so sad? Always   so   sad
Afraid of life, death, hell and the grave
And any sight of shadow
Had I been able to come to you - in my contrition come to you
And burned, in that hallowed place,
Sacrifice changing caustic essential truth . . .
We are   all dying!
We are all dying . . . and of late I dream
Those dreams that call me back to undone things . . .
Anger rides them.   Anguish.   Seldom, if ever, is there joy
And this woman mourns memory

Wondering why wonder if there'll come a season of meaning.
God of my mourning hour
Had I been a bit more able to taste grief
And still touch love and hold my faith
     In a faithless world.
Daybreak's about. Without voices dance in mist
Blissfully children rise to Grannies bakin bread
And the rod not spared.

Let me continue . . .
Open my mind . . .
Climb in my heart   .
Infiltrate thought   .
     Prone to wander reckless in the dark
         Apart from the shadow of your heart.

BETWIXT and BETWEEN

PREDICAMENT
Perfection
In The Beginning: GOD!
Perplexity
In The Beginning: GOD…?

SILK SCREEN

Did you make the clouds, God?
Or is all I see
The accumulation of gases and pollution
Against eternity
And not divine silhouettes of color - dark
Below light and all
Upon an eternal blackboard
Perfect perpetual movements
Turning on themselves
Spinning thought to and fro
God . . . did you know such into being . . . or
Shall I suspect another?

YOU WHO STAYED

You hold out for meanin
Refuse to go screamin in ballpark-frenzy
Fanning flames to Hezekiah Walker walkin ya
To the throne and Cleveland callin' ya
      In call response.
You know the notes. Had the tunes play ya. . .lift ya
From sittin down on the stool-o-do-nothin feelin
Got you realin in the sanctuary
Rememb'rin' last night's passion as a whip of penance.
God-a-mighty know a body can go for only sooooooooo long
      Lackin touch.
So lay you down. . .slay you in the spirit
Spit and spew demons and let them dance and prance
And cough and speak in a gruff voice "we are in control"
Be a child hidin in the corner
While the deacons shoo the young away
'N have them say of you when you are old . . .
You are the one who stayed . . .
      And was jumped on.

AS THE LEAF

If you tell me the answers
I will ask you the questions
And when you answer that
I will ask of you another and another and another
So Soothe if you might this consternation
Apply any balm to it
There'll be another potion and another notion
And another day of angst.
Tell me your story
And I'll tell you mine
Gather your gods by your right side
And mine . . . I'll assemble to my left
And let them banter their supremacy
And let them set their lines of demarcation
And we'll then see who stands
      As the smoke rises.

Sing your song long from the terraced pinnacle
Of your certitude . . .
While in the low country
      Among the folk
           Among the people
Without steeple or chance
I will dance the dance of my unknowing
. . . And the eyes of the crowd
Will cry their "me eithers"
And the souls of the people in that truth
Will bend Godward as the leaf bends
To the light
      Of the son.

DAMASCUS

Like Paul on the road,
I thought Damascus was mine
One night on my knees - Mother B interpreting tongues
God spoke to me. He did!
Didn't tell me to go preach or sell all I had
To feed the poor. I was poor in my own spirit then.
Didn't tell me sing or go to seminary
Or join the Sisters of Mercy
Didn't say make way to Mecca
Or surround Jericho seven times till the wall come tumblin
Didn't ask for sacrifice of my first born upon a slab
Awaitin his stay of hand with ram in bush.
It's just absent the whirlwind
'n absent the noise
'n absent the mass choir from the church
Of who-doin-what-to-whom
He simply say - He did!
I don't leave and I don't forsake!
But . . . me? I always wanted it ALL
Lights!
     Camera!
          Action!
God in technicolor and Panavision - surround-sound
Down from Sinai knockin me about
'n takin me out of my own destruction.
I didn't want to work for it.
I wanted God to get off his seat of do nothin
And do somethin God-awesome
To let niggas know he would kick ass

And kick ass some more.
But, He just wink and He say - He did
He just wink and He say -
"I'm walkin wid ya baby!"

STILL RUNNING

I'm still running, God.
What I really wanted was you . . .
Clear. Simplistic. Personal.
Not this second-hand
Hand-me-down Jesus you've become
Offered by so much educated rhetoric
Left-over from some other person's
Estimation of your existence. I want my own!
So. No. I can't be at the women's day celebration - lost
In white dresses and red carnations
And the March birthday day group can do without me
Cause I don't care if we don't collect more money
Than the birthday group for February
And I cannot,
Repeat - I cannot march Jericho-circled
Around this church
Singing "I don't feel no-ways tired,"
Cause God I am tired.
      Weary.
           Spent.
               Exasperated
By these hide and seek games we play you and I.
Can't we stop? You put away that awesome Gods-man-ship
-
Terrible and distant.
Me - put away my flight - determined
Never to be caught.

FACE TO FACE

When I was a child, God
They told me You did it all
They never said a thing about gases and pollution
Forming the color in clouds
They never mentioned Darwin and some monkey
Cancer and TB or death and dying classes
No one every explained the theory of relativity . . .
Relative, that is, to enough power
To blow the hold damn world away.
They said you spoke
And it was so
That you commanded . . .
And it all came into being.
They never spoke of the pain of ostracism
Or the loneliness of aging
Nor pondered the philosophy of which is worse
Only that you cared
And died
And was coming again.

They said nothing of Sahel's child
Belly distended arms threadbare
Or Jake - fat-assed, laid-back junkie
In some housing project in DC
Peddling his own scheme of death.

They never once said, yes . . . but!
Yes   but there are ambiguities
Yes   but there are gray areas in between

That you could make love
And not love. That you could just want to be held
And not give one hot damn
Whether he's got honorable intentions or no.
They state only right or wrong
Yea or nay
Cause every other song is evil.

They never mentioned longing.
They said, "Come out from among them
And be separate."
They failed to note
Soul wanting communion with soul,
Spirit with spirit
And that many times you get sick
Kissing up to the white-robed preacha
With the white-robed choir
And the ushers with the hats
      With the tassels on the left.
And that maybe
You want to know what souls' drink
At the corner bar
Or the philosophy of the neighborhood prostitute.

I keep wanting to meet You, face-to-face
Adult to Creator.
God, yes You said be child-like in faith,
In peace and love.
But, I am a woman
Trying to pull it all together
      To see You through barriers
           To break down partitions
                To make sense - out of no sense

And in the midst of harrowing indications to the contrary
To be one with You and my fellowman.
And if all ecclesiastical disciplines disappear, God
At least . . . to be one with myself.

BETWIXT AND BETWEEN

Here, betwixt and between
I mean no disrespect
But keep covenant with none, and am the one
      Spewed
From the mouth of God.

I find it hard to acquiesce assurance:
You, but not you   .
Not you, but you …Who can say?
Who can say which way worlds formed
Or if storms blow wild and free
From God's fingertips
Brushed across the face of sea.

Who can say?

Here in permanent moderation
I haven't oath or creed
Or special day or way I say a prayer
      No talisman holds nightmare
No regal air propels to papal audience.
Here in the half and half
'n maybe so and could be
Angels may not dance
And heaven and hell's a chance meeting
On a midnight newsbreak.
You who court deity for the sake of beating death
So sure beyond surety
But, say you yay

Or say you nay
Shall you return again to tell?

In this hallowed ambiguity . . . God dwells
Ancient and fixed upon the turbulence
Mincing neither word nor deed
Weeding through the mire of impotent desire
To ultimate truth . . .
Is there any?
Come. Come into this mystery with me
See with unmasked eye
Taste and smell and feel real meaning.
The only absolute is death:
Oblivion crammed in the mouth of babes
And old-folk on the brink sinking
To that going away
Stay with me God
Hold my hand
And help me understand my madness.

IF IT WEREN'T FOR DEATH

If it weren't for death
I suppose I wouldn't be afraid - chastising God
Putting the rod to his back
For lack of imagination on things eternal.
Death ain't a good thing
Not a well, everybody's doing it thing
Not a won't you come too thing
Not a try it, you'll like it thing
       And if you don't we'll call it off thing.
Scoff at it. Harangue it. Scream at it from nightmare
       Swear and spit
And pit it to the madness of the crowd
Though none's allowed your tragedy but you
And you will go despite protest
Or posturing for delay.

Today, if it weren't for death
Perhaps I'd care a little more
Laugh louder more
Turn teary eyed expression into rain
Washing pain more
Gain some elevated meaning
Gleaning from absolute knowledge - absolute absolution.
This is what I know
I've been here fifty years
My fears not mitigated by time
And that silly hide 'n seek
Is weakening me as we speak.

Tweak my soul
Put a message in my heart
Tell me something bold and good to dispel fear.
I asked my ma about death when I was four
Though she bore me no ill will, I suppose
Her laughter to my face took whatever grace
Apportioned me.

And being old
All I see is earth and worms
And little steepled people telling me lies
Trying not to scream or seem unruly.
But, truly, what a hand handed us
And no one to cuss at for it
I'm a little tired feigning smiles
When all the while death is naming names
And I have a train to catch.

POSITIVE SELF-TALK

I do positive self-talk like I was told.
Don't languish in that place absent grace
With what if, why and maybe.
Lately I count to nine for time
To find high meaning with the folk of answers
My questions are placed in foil for safety
And reason coiled about doubt
And the shout of the crowd for silence.
If I had a genie, I'd call him
If Yoruba would free me, I would dance
If Holy Ghost hoe-down led me down the path to sanity
I would'a stayed in the sanctuary singing.
But . . . there's a ringing in me
Low and repetitious - omniscient of my lack.
I am wanting back to the waters
From where I came before they named me
"you who will not know . . . and so goes on lonely".
Oh, I'm no different from the rest
Wanting the calm along the way
Wanting yay or nay or never
Wanting like-minded soul bold beside me
Boasting faith folded in my arms.
But . . . I can't be charmed
I've seen the other side of knowing
Absent reason . . .
Well, this be the season of what's real
And I am still here talking positively
Positively assured
There really are no answers.

GOD MUST KNOW

I think God must know
More than I know
And so this show of hands and stands
Declaring what I should feel
With the zeal my mama said was steady and true
Will get you little notice.

God ain't for obscure worship
Wants the tenth and the shout
And no one on the out still figuring at fifty.

I think God must have seen me then
Small . . . not thinking much at all
But seeing holocaust and loss as primal.

The angels came. My name was tossed
Like the last one chosen for track
And I can't give back that sighting.

I am writing this cause word won't come untainted
And all my sainted folk are gone
And while they did no harm (if you don't count nightmare)
The air be thick in this soul-space
And grace would come except it can't find room
     Or footing.

I was a special needs baby
Not marked with limp or sty
But a knowing from the first a curse obtained

And I'd no arsenal or brew
To shoo demons back
And they attack with pride.
Well I've cried enough
And heard enough
And seen enough to know
It was never my show . . .
And all this rage is staged
And the play - almost over.

GOD CALLS

Acid pain
Bare pain
Cradles in places
Daring
Exposure
From this lack
God calls
Hale and Hardy
Instigating
Journeys to reason
Kindly send my regrets,
Lamentably,
More is
Needed here
Oblivious
Perturbing
Questions quickly
Resolved
Sends seeker
To total terror.
Understand this
Veiled doubt
Works no magic
Xercise no restraint
Yes,
Zap it!

THOUGHTS AFTER A NIGHT OF DEPRESSION
(With Appropriate Pleading)

Why are we dying?
An apple, a garden, a choice
A voice calling through the mist
Where are you? And one - insisting the other
Is the culprit?
One piece of fruit and eternity is off
And labor and death enter and control
While we march each to our own ending
Defending faith born of fear.

Why are We dying, anyway?
An angel fell - his cohorts with him
Cause God had an "oops" moment
And from there to eternity
We shoulder the warfare for things
We did not do?
And while I lay on the altar tending my regret
I am beset with the notion
That God left long ago on a voyage
Knowing answers He's not going to give
And as I live I know only these questions:
Who arbitrated this agreement?
Who set upon papyrus absolutes
For which there are no absolutes we can fathom really?
Who among the thousands of witnesses holds truth
Above all truth and tells it plain and simple
For the common folk to know a God of love -
His yoke calm and easy

Without the sleazy fear of death and hell
Looming as the backdrop to all there is
And ever will be?

See - when I tell them God is a God of love and he wouldn't
They say He is a God of wrath and he does what he does.

When I say He knew things all beforehand and he coulda,
    He shoulda,
They say who are you to charge creation and creator
Who are you to say what God must do to be God?
Well He could'a wiped out Death!

Why are we dying?
A shroud. a cramped box, a dirge
Ascending the descending hill to oblivion,
Why are we the beneficiaries of creation-in-situ
Sprung into malignant emaciations of soul?

Shs! Keep this to yourself
Don't tell anyone
Stash it in a chiferobe rolled
Into a sachet scarf - and forget it
Make sure the members of the Presbytery \
    Don't get wind of it
Make sure my grandma don't know
For she is one of switches for sacrilege
And even from the ridge of heaven
She will break a branch and strike a stripe for hell.
Don't tell my lover, Joe
Or my sisters - the Pentecostal reverends

Rallying the banner for righteousness, rigidity and remorse.
Of course - Don't tell the children
Don't interrupt their play
And have them say "but, momee, but, but, but momee"
Then scuttle them away quoting chapter and verse
Rehearsed but making no sense or reason.
Shs! Don't tell a soul
That even now, that I am old
I still badger God 'bout purpose
And am bored with boilerplate answers
Grandfathered in from men
In designer suits and Rolex.

Just why are We dying?
The voice of one crying in the wilderness
Came to us heralding the light that would outshine
      The darkness.
He was for life
Yet the world wants death and is charmed
By the agony of its people posted and paraded
On the evening news at seven.

In this apologetic theme
I redeem Him (I REDEEM HIM?) Yes,
      I redeem HIM from responsibility.
See, I have seen the enemy
      And it is I (That old cliché)
My hope plastered to the side of my bed
Praying that in the night
The sickle will miss the head of a fool
Blabbering!
Umph!
(There is more to *this* poem).

GOOD TIME MUSIC

They play,
Good-time music
Holy, good-time music
And I dance in circular motion
Beating invincible, invisible demons
Praise God!
If I can boogie,
      I ought to dance the holy dance.
But, boogying's unconditional
You don't have to do no soul searching
      To boogie
So when the good-time music's played
You just strut yo stuff.

THE ONE WHO DANCED

There was the one who danced
      In the sanctuary
Gathering the frowns about her
From out her came tongues of fire
For she was higher than spirit.
We were children then - when Bessie danced
Glancing our "Motha Whys?"
      Silenced by the "shush chile" of her eyes
While she danced.
Her strut was nothing less than jazz
Hyped in honky-tonk-razz-ma-tazz
      And Holy Ghost hoe down magic.
How tragic now this finer stance
That will not laugh, or sing . . . or dance.

CONVERSATION WITH GOD
(With Analogous Apposite Annotations)

I love the Lord
He heard my cry
And pitied every groan
Long as I live
And trouble rise
I'll hasten to his throne.

                              Traditional.

I love the Lord?
Well, maybe I do, and then maybe . . .
Most times I can't even figure out who you are God
Or what to call you.
I suppose I could keep it simple
Call you Jesus . . . My grand-mama did.
Or, in that stead, do I call you Allah
Like Aunt Helen from Philly
With the white drape about her head
Who everybody said was just a little different
(if you know what I mean).
My old man's folk from Car-o-Iina
Knows a whole lotta who-do about voodoo
But I tends to makes myself scarce from that scene
Seeing as dey into graveyard dust, chicken bones,
      And potent potions from wayward kin.
Well, then do I call you Buddha or Laotse or Confucius
Or the force wid me
Or - Just HE . . ..

He who surrounds eternity
He for whose pleasure all things were created
He who openeth and no man shutteth
With the sharp sword with two edges
Whose eyes are a flame of fire
With the wooly head and bronze toes
Who white folk sho-nuf knows just can't be black.
Does I know for a fact…that You's a he.
He . . . he . . . he . . . he . . . he. . . he . . . he. What about a she?
What…about…a…she?
SHEEEeee. . . who nourishes
SHEEEeee. . . who stands in the gap and from her lack
Is able to leap tall buildings wid a single bound
Then. . .hit the ground groovin wid her man wid one hand
And sooth in her chil'ren wid the other.

And, tell me this. . . my Brotha,
You say. . .You heard my cry?
Well…when they was sacrificin' babies and virgins
And the purest and holiest and most innocent of things
Did you hear them crying? Did it matter that they cried?
Did you hear the cry of my people in middle-passage
Mashed in one another's vomit and waste.
Did you taste the blood from the mastah's lash
Or hear virginity ripped from the hip
Of pre-pubescent girls
When our fathers and brothers and lovers swayed
As fruit on willow trees, our mothers sinking to their knees
Did you note that tear.
Did you hear my weepin…in the death camps at Auschwitz
Did you hear my weepin…in the death camps at Cambodia

Did you hear my weepin…in the death camps at Angola
Or in Jackson or Watts or Selma,
      Or Seventh Street, Washington, D. C.
Did you hear me, God?
Did you hear my cry…that night
When pride and heart and soul were counted irrelevant
Did you hear his chant whispered over and over in my ear
"Can't tell yo mama, can't tell yo mama, can't tell yo mama"
Till death itself could not have silenced fear!
God…did you hear…and pity every groan.

In the midnight when somebody's holding me
And I reach through flesh to touch eternity
And in the pit of that longing I cry out – Yes! YES!
God, will you bless that joining in the morning light?
Suppose God, we ain't rightly married
And he ain't rightly mine
Or he ain't rightly propertied
Or rightly educated
Or a member of the right church or family
Suppose God, he ain't rightly a member of nothin at all.
Now, I knows it's your Call. But, pity?
I don't want no pity. I   don't   want   no   pity!
I just Want You to get back to Yo business
And leave me to my business.
Leave me … to my lovin
'n let me hold this man
And not repent …
      Or regret when it's over.
And it's over soon enough?

Long as I live? Hump!
What a joke. What a f-'n joke
Three-score and ten and if by reasonable measure . . .
Maybe four - Be real! Get real!
Here, You stretch from eternity to eternity
From everlasting to everlasting
And You throw seventy years this way
Saying, "one day in My sight
Is as a thousand years". Well I ain't You
And I say. . . death. . . and earth. . .and worms
Is death   and earth. . . and worms
Nah, buddy You can't squirm outta this one.
Ain't no use to apologize.

Cause, God, trouble do rise.
And you think I don't know trouble
Well, I tell you I know trouble
And I know you ain't always been
Where you supposed to be
Tendin to things you supposed to be tendin to
When it do come.
Like when Michael committed suicide
Big bullet hole in the crevice of his head
    Sos I know he dead
His body limp…lingering on a slab
And on that cab ride from Sicklerville
I grab…his personal effects…get this -
His personal effects -
Cigarettes, a journal, a wallet
And, tucked politely away in wool-tweed pocket
A pack of Lifesavers . . .
A f"n pack . . . of Lifesavers.

And you still say
I should make way to your throne.
Your throne? YOUR throne?
Your throne. . .I suppose, be big, bold
And bedecked with gold and precious stone
Wid you alone sittin wid your homies
Sayin whose to come and whose to go. . .
And. . . I know I can't fake it.
Cause, I sit here, even now, I sit here
Older, wiser, stronger
Not understandin a damned thing bout nothin
Not believin nothin all the way
Not acceptin nothin all the way
And really, God
Not given to sayin, 'Yea Lord, hallelujah, amen"
When. . .what I really mean - is maybe. Maybe?

Hey You! HE. . .who surrounds eternity
And is the head Negro in charge. . .so I been told
How do I know…if I have gained the whole world?
How do I know…if I have lost my soul?

OK. You win. I surrender!
I know that tender minds can't comprehend
The who. . .or where. . .or when. . .. of what you are
I simply pray. . .that on that starship where you rule
You hold some kingly mercy. . .
      For a fool!

JUBILLEE

When the praises rang
The people in the pews went wild
Crazy wild
Like they did in juke joint days
In the aisle
To the beat of bishop booming
Big bold heaven words
Calling us all from silence
Sitting like God was stone.
When the parish prayed
The people on their feet felt sway
They swayed
The way they did to the chant of drum
The low hum
Of deacon pleading passions-
Praying us from silence
Sitting like God was deaf.
When they all spoke in tongues of fire
     Like fire
The people swept /leapt to the sound
Of Sia-He-Com-A-Sia
And the pyre burned bright
As the mountain of God
Speaking us from silence
Sitting like God was mute.
When the choir sang
And, Oh, they sang
And mourned in cadence
Of a funeral dirge

And forged high sound from weary breast
To the boom of organ dreams
      And timbrels.
Calling us from silence
Sitting like God had no song.

HE COMES

He comes to fill this place in me
That was it ripe for the filling
No one else could fill anyway
Neither being able to nor willing
To wind and wade in the watery mist
Insisting that beneath it lay that pearl
Worth more than what is seen.

He speaks to my contradictions
My lust for life often overriding my desire to praise
Even through the misty hazed-over glassy spaces
Even through the stations I have crossed
Again and again
Thinking to make right what cannot be right
Or slightly bent heavenward.

He comes into this empty chamber
Fixing Himself beside me
As he fixes Himself in me
Knowing the hardening of hearts
And the masks
And the tasks we ask of ourselves but cannot do
Oh - - if we but only knew
The simple limitations of flesh surrounding soul.

I suspect grace is a word
For us sauntering in the hinterland
Stepping over chards and mind-fields
Hopeful that what we reach for

Be not image without form or substance
And that subsequent footsteps might be easier
And a little lighter
Actually leading to a place of recovery . . .
Recovery!
Not even joy. . .That's an oxymoron now
But, just recovery enough to say
I'm still in the game and it's my turn.

I burn with desire to hold God near
And not fear you or the world
     Or media of mass communications
        Or addictions for and to pain
           Or naming over and over and over again
The reason for my stoic face
While really, asking why the others of you are laughing
And wishing I had your laughter
Knowing…in a world pushing Armageddon. . .
Laughter's 'bout as needed now
As a new immuno-deficient retrovirus.
Weep with me children.

He still comes nigh
Often in a voice or whisper
Rarely parading his majesty
Asking me to keep things simple
And just let it be, Let It Be, LET IT BE!
And see the mystery of salvation
Often tucked
     Between me and the windstorm
        Between me and the doily moving in memory

Across my Grandma's armchair
      Between me and a whisper of never leaving
Or forsaking
Asking me to come on back
So He can fill those places
      Ripe for the filling.

PROPHECY

I thought your coming was prophecy:
That somewhere during our tribulation
There would be a meeting of souls in transit
As you lit the night sky leaving lesser gods
In your smoke.
You spoke of the eternal
And paths joining for more beneficent benefactor.
You were the arch angel of my pleasure
The high exalted potentate of my pain.
Was there some gain to this love?
Knowing we were juxtaposed between worlds
And the whirling wind would bend us
Breaking to pieces our momentous synchronicity.
The simple thing was this:
That we would meet and kiss and go on lonely
Owning the path to our own destiny
Knowing we could not please it - and - us
And all the other harbingers of need.
If I could plead my cause
I'd have you pause and see beyond the smile
Of this longing and this want for touch.
Much more obtains:
My years of waiting absent the confederation of the holy
My years of being
My years of knowing summers
Counted on the tips of my fingers and toes
Only to have run out of both twice over
And then some years more. . .
I had hoped - your arms would beat back death

I had hoped you'd sprinkle liquid laughter
And have the dance tune tuned toward our passion
And perdition be of another universe or clime. . .

I'm a hard sell on prophets now
Those who gaze and see
And decree what cannot be
As we walk weary toward our entropy.

Everything ends.
Everything bends back into the bowels of earth
- Mother of our birth and dark receptacle
Of the shell we leave behind -
There is none of our kind able to rescind
Or tend the garden of this fear.

But, there was one:
When we had seen the stuff of our shame
When we'd grown tired of this tribulation
When all we knew was this tribulation
When we had silenced praise and let the sacrifices
Rot in chambers and the embers flickered
For lack of tending
When we were sending tenders to false gods
And had lost our way and the roads traveled were sealed
Against our homecoming
When we had had enough
When the world was weary with weeping
And the children needed to see
And believe and receive
Hope higher that mortality.

When the fullness of time had come
When there was nowhere to look but up
Toward majesty excellent and fair
Yea, there was ONE. . .
    And he was the SON. . .
        Of GOD!

THE MOURNERS' BENCH

COMPARING NOTES

Who
Was the first for you, he pled?
Then sensing I held no coy reply
He viewed the un-
earthing of my dead
And shrank from the
terror in my eye
Then . . . bowed low
In crimson pillows on our bed
I simply said . . .
"It was rape!"

SPOTTSYLVANIA LEGACY

It was never really home!
Not a soul place
But I stood, by whatever grace
Voyeur to alien conversation and circumstance
Not intended for these ears and eyes.
They'd be surprised to know I noticed.
Noticed and retained
Names, dates, nuance, hook and line -
Verbatim palpable apathy preserved in stone
Though time has blown a mean dream on 'em.
There was never a private hug
Never a honey don't cry
And the lullaby. . .a forced scoop
Of soggy oats and a Betty- Boop cartoon.
Jesus was what you did on Sunday, I suppose,
But, Monday was a different day
For daddy's bent on beatings
And leaving poisons placed about for eyes and hands
Too small to comprehend real evil.
I have known a long time now, how it was then
But, send for the old folk and they're all mute
So there's no resolute remedy for this tragedy.
See: there are two people in this poem
She remembering and recording
Hoarding pain as rain in a Spotsylvania kettle,
And she of mettle and brawn who even in grave sorrow
Is strong in her resolve
That tomorrow they are all absolved . . .
    Their ignorance.

SENSELESS FIRE

Go away you fool
I wanted reason to wake
Other than I'd passed night fitful
And sun was not kind enough to hide
A little longer
Sun's got its own desire
Spreading senseless fire on deadness.
Guess what I know
Figure what I'd say
Walking to the face of sun
Bold in bright clothes
So I wouldn't get heat stroke
Know what I'd tell that well of luminous goo
Go way, you fool! No light here.
Only dark memory and old folk
Waiting to die.
And I am tired pulling them
One strand at a time to light
Only to have them melt
      And slither down
Dripping darkness all over me.

THE WOE OF A CHILD

It would'a made more sense
To leave me there
In the peace of the water
And let the sound of your breath
Calm me like a breeze.
I should'a stayed in the heart of God
And listened to the beat, boom, beat
Of angels' feet dancing. I am not for this place!
In his disgrace
I am the chance my father took in a drunken stupor
That neither he nor she knew what to make of later.
I am the reason she called him, bastard,
'n told his mama he was no good
And she had ruined him for any woman.
He said of her, "bitch, go slow" -
And the blow to her belly taught me
To steel myself for pain.
I can taste her smoke
Smell her gin, hear her whispered dream
Of "God let it die"
As if I weren't soul within a brief borrowed house.
I came into the world, then,
Eyes wide and able to discern spirits
And spirits of a clever sort roamed my room
And motioned me wise beyond my day. . .
You can't play having known eternity at birth
And truth perched upon the mantel, crying.
When I am old and of no use to anyone
Save nursing home ledgers and vultures for the dead

That I have said these things
Will cause no warp in collective unconscious . . .
I have seen demons and gods laughing
And. . . he woe of a child - stuffed in a battered box
    Of memory.

FAULT

My words shut down long ago.
I decided not to speak for fear of truth
Spewing forth unstoppable.
I was hurt in places I was taught I didn't even own . . .
(having been owned by everyone; the boy next door
My peoples' friends and strangers.)
I was surprised to learn that horded
In a space I called "don't touch"
I lived and died a hundred tries to understand why,
In any event, it even made a difference.
I wasn't pretty. thin, or white . . .
. . .Yet, a finger pierced my child body
And mired in that trespass, the truth of other sins.
My grandmother's slap told me it was me. My fault.
It's you. Your fault. God punishes. It's you.
So in her old age, I stay away
And shun the voice of God. . .
It's you, It's you, It's you, it's you, it's you, it's you,
it's you, it's you, it's you, it's you, it's you, it's you It's you,
it's you, it's you, it's you. . .it's you . . .
it's you. . .it's you. . .

HARRIET TUBMAN

I would'a been afraid if I were she,
Harriet Tubman,
I would'a been afraid, but, I would'a gone anyway!
I would' a gone through white folk wid dogs
I would'a got up. Even bitchin' I would'a got up
And made my way, and had my say
For freedom.

I did for my children.
When she said to me - "he hurt me"
And they said, "well, he repented at the altar"
I didn't say seven hail-marys, forgive him
Nothin was full of grace
And every crime of ashen betrayal
Pushed back into his face.

See, I got up and I told them
See, I got up and made a fool of my passivity
Not this time, I said.
Not this time.

My motha was afraid 'n she chose not to know
What she had to know
And so they came . . . pillaged . . . and ravaged.

It was about Janey
And the blood -
My grand-ma took me to Mother B to be accused
And my mama neva said a word. Though I knew she heard

Though I knew that it wasn't me
Knew more had happened to my six-year old friend
Than she skinned herself against a jagged wall
I knew it was all horrible:
The larger horror was
Was that I - was expendable.

I still get up.
I still get up
And tomorrow I will get up
And go out anyway - God willing -
Wonder if I'll find Janey. Find the truth - my truth
Like Harriet Tubman found the road to freedom.

WHAT THE ANGER FEELS LIKE

Your stare reminds me
Your empty stare reminds me that you are wounded
And because you are wounded
Then my pain is of no consequence
I learn to say I need nothing
And my flare for hiding things
Is the hell
Of my insanity.

Your words are full of venom
Your words remind me you are angry
And because you are angry
Then my disappointment
My hot seeded rage at your trespass
Is shut in silence.
I learn to turn eyes downward
So I won't invoke the hell
Of your insanity.

Your fists remind me
For you are strong
And black eyes your specialty
(Ain't it handy the things you can cover with rouge)!
But, your fists remind me
That anything I feel
Needs be wrapped in tissue
And tucked politely away
Unless I stir the demon in us both
And one of us . . .
      Dies.

JESSE'S BROWN

Jesse's pine tree
Grows in a white pot near my window
By my chair.
That chair, wood-brown with tan padded-seating
And lighter browns scalloped across its back
Just brown, battered and bruised
The way 'used' things be.
It was one of four
Bought at a flea-market the year Jesse was here
      And left
Him gone . . . I remember now . . .
He supposed them a steal at twenty-bucks a throw
But I know they were just old chairs
Old chairs we could' a jewed them for
Had he ceased his cry of castrating Black bitchiness.
However, that was Jesse
Paying well to veil his need of me
Wanting me, silenced in sick subservience.
I couldn't kneel.
Since then, I've seen him once or twice, -
No three times -
Once: I sought him to reason his going
And he hugged me to himself
In goodbye.
Once he came for my car - "for purposes of nation building"
And I wondered - though I didn't say it then-
"NEGRO, you want what . . . for what." I was just like that
      Sometimes.
Then . . . then there was yesterday; his woman-dreaded

And he appropriately Afrocentric-ly-attired
I admired him so - his look, his youth
And with what air he sought me
Through the crowded room in hello.
Old friends should stop. and speak of this
      Or that trite pleasantry
And plant a kiss on used brown things -
Where the bruises use to be!

THE MOURNERS' BENCH

If I had known . . .
What I was mourning for
Then the mourners' bench
Would'a been the seat of sweet release -
They said it was
Instead of the chair
Where I met descendent demons -
And spewed them forth
In spit and incantations.
If I had known
I could have screamed -
Screamed homage to my wounded child
I should' a never went as a sinner
I should'a never swayed
Under some other body's guilt
I should'a never prayed for forgiveness
For a child - Mine -
Innocent and lost.
I should'a hurled accusations
I should'a made them know my anger
I should'a called God's wrath
On the bastards - of my abuse.
Then, I could'a left the mourners' bench . . .
      SAVED!

PURGE

You begin to rid yo' set of dese demons.
Though dey come screamin
Though dey come screamin
Though yo house is swept clean -
And dey come screamin
Bringin sev'n others wid dem . . .
You begin to let dem go.
You know dey ain't yo demons.
You know you ain't responsible
You know that is it over
And you no longer live
In that hell handed you in gold sparklin wrap.
And since dey ain't yo demons . . .
You give em back!

BLURRED PHOTOGRAPHS

. . . Lying in dark chiferobes
Like the one Daddy kept in his room
Under lock and key
And only he granted entrance.

MOTOWN MELODIES

The tired has come before the dark
Our evensong - gone from boogie to blue
And who we knew is fixed in funeral parlor ledgers
Naming those in attendance
Our bodies shutting down
Time's running through our veins
And youth reclaimed is a dream
Obscured by Insulin and Demerol
And stalling by the way to catch our breath.
There's not been a day of late of springtime word
      Woven in and out
And our shouts of hallelujah
Be gibberish as we name our griefs dropping
      From the branch.

Our souls are old as earth
Birth from us - death to us
And the fuss from the 'amen corner' is causing much distraction.
All of our folk are thinned
And penning names in war worn scripture
Does not endure us much to God.
And...Yet...God trods here none the less.
 So I'd best keep these groanings to myself.

... All things move and change
Turn and burn themselves down to dust
Our minds loose minute detail -
A face...a name

A gesture - one particular
As the thumbing of my mother's hands at table
One. . .rubbing the other in "there-there" consolation.
Our hearts, and must we speak of this,
But, yes, our hearts have kissed
So many good-bye's and fare-the wells
That we live to tell of it is gift.

Here. . .in this shadow place
Grace and pain reign in royal ambiguity

And I'd tell you, if I could, where to put the Band-Aid stripe
And what tear was wont most for the wiping.
But, I was never weaned of hope
And hope dies hard in the heart of a seeker
Daring to hold on.

So, Come - Come and sit a spell
And let's not dwell on eternity
Or ask the host to run this once again
We've other things to ponder -
Love,
        Laughter,
                Liquid sunsets
Mellowing in the arc of the new moon.
We've babies to bless
        And festival a-comin
To our hummin of Motown melodies.

BLURRED PHOTOGRAPHS

Her features chiseled. Her chin broad and square.
Her hair - shimmering -
Brushed from a widow's peak - balled at the nape
      Of her neck. She was regal!
When I was young - lookin' at me - then lookin' at her
They'd say, "Tave, how did that happen?"
Then she'd pat me - tell me, "don't mind them folk no mind"
But, every fo' church day, she'd have her say
Ketch that hair up some-kinda way
To press the kink out/and curl the curl in -
Cause saints couldn't see her grandbabies
Lookin' nappy.

She was soap and water for saddle-socks
Scoured on scrub-board lain in four poster bath
The draft from Granny's room piercing Saturday bath-time
ways
Scrubbin' kick-ball scum and runs from neighbor boys
And them eyes of hers stoppin' that switch
      And hitch in yo skirt . . .
Show in' your business.

She was switches from walnut branches
Avalanching green-brown bombs squashing squirrels
And beds of gladioli and green bitter grapes.
Time was a long time comin, then.
Weeks were months. Months, years.
She wasn't old then – takin' us on trips to Luray
And New York Harbor for a day on a tug boat

'n fixin potato salad for Deacon Berry who drove the bus.

There were rats in her garage. Not mice. Rats.
She didn't pay them rats no neva mind
She'd send us to dump trash
And pull the rake for fall.
Didn't like rats. Didn't know nobody who did
But the trash had to go
And the leaves had to go
And she weren't about no do-nothin girls -
Women had to be' bout women's work.

Twice a week the ice-man come
And set the chunks beneath the stairwell
Then Daddy chopped them small
Sent out the call to fill his thermos' full
To be brought to his room:
Two of water, two of Trim diet-soda, two of beer.
Every night.
Two of water, two of Trim diet-soda, two of beer.
     Every night.
His diabetic legs turned purple
And Aunt Teresa bathed his sores in her home-made brew
But, death wasn't fooled.

When Granny died - we cried.
     In the aisles of the Rehoboth saints say,
"Laugh, when they die, and cry when they born."
That's all they knew to guide us through
The death of our granny who we slept with -
Who sang us songs and rocked us.

Aunt Olivia came from Spotsylvania and fried chicken.
Sport - the great white dog
Failed to see that funeral food was for people.
She gave him all of it.
Uncle Buddy humped the door with Sissy behind it
Humped it like some 14th street whore
And wonders why we grimace at his touch.

Mama moved to an apartment on 4th street.
I stuffed myself till I retched Campbell's beans,
Hot dogs, grape Kool-Aid, and Butter-Pecan by Bryers.
      I felt better.
I held a little girl while my neighbor put a hot match
To her flesh - (A match-print raw against her thigh) -
I didn't tell my mama -
Her mama didn't tell my mama --
Ain't never heard no mo' sense --
Ain't never said no mo' sense.
      I dream.

Mama moved again. After that Jimmy was her boyfriend.
Then the African. Then Sergeant Anderson.
Then Mr. Joe and Horace and Ike (the Gambler).
And Mr. Gross. And Mr. White. And Lonny.
And one, whose name escapes me, drove for Bobby Kennedy.
Mr. Gross smothered a White lady in Georgetown.
      Lonny was a rapist.
           Lonny was my rapist!

I ain't old yet, but, they all gone . . .
Granny. Daddy. Olivia.
And even my mama before mother
Then mother herself - - and folk I try to name
Their faces blurred on photographs I forgot to mark
Lyin in dark chiferobes
      Like the one Daddy kept in his room under lock and key
And only he - granted entrance.

I was hopin Mama lied that time she laughed
      At my fear of death.
Now, I know the laugh was desperation
I seen it since. Seen it in her eyes
Felt it round her death-bed
And wanted to apologies
For not understanding. . .AII…Those…Years.
I wanted to laugh then -
She would' a got the Joke.
Nobody else could'a.
      You had to be there.

SOLID

Yesterdays were solid
Knowing things my mama held
To hold sanity.
Not long after her fall to madness
I began to know marshy spaces
My footsteps slipping low
To places where the dark-ones refused silence.
In her words
I had craved the certainty of life to life
But. . . she stooped in the mall
Screaming Lord have mercy, Lord, Have Mercy
And, not man nor god moved
To sooth her agony;
And my charge of nothing -
    Nothing more -
Bore new birth.
Death is no friend to the faithless
And life's not kind
To those whose mama's fall
    To madness.

FATHER MEMORY...

NOTHING!
NOTHING!

...WHO CANNOT SPEAK of OUR FATHERS

For those of us who cannot speak
Of our fathers. Not even to place face
To bad memory - to say for shame, for shame
He was philanderer or fool
Or drooled in his supper given a stiff Bacardi.
For those who cannot recall a voice
Or hear a voice or song floating
From misted shower. And have no flowered way
He use to send us courting.
For those sauntering
Where there was no ear for keeping secrets,
Or pockets picked for penny pitchings
And pictures posted sacredly about to scatter demons.
For those who have sought in every man's arm
And every man's bed that thread from yesterday
To now…and now...to tomorrow:
Let's speak this sorrow kind
And mind you - there be no righteous word
To mask such death in softer-loud
Nor pretty shroud to wrap it fit
      For the viewing.

FATHER...

Enter at risk
My birth is noble as mother earth
And worth the distanced traveled from your sun
To find me.
Come - embrace this issue of your loins
Watch - My face is yours
My eyes, my body shape exactly you
I am your mother/sister
And every woman you have held
Hoping my mother's fragrance faded
Hoping her song was silenced in shattered nightscape.
Ever wonder why
I hold you long since fatherhood absconded
Nothing held in hand
Is more than nothing turned away!
I see you there
And could despair your pathologies
But, I see you there
And know it was not I, but you
Who lacked the will
      To love.

I DO NOT HUG MY SISTER

I do not hug my sister
No…we enter celebration and cast a parallel eye
And her chaps and mine are kind
In joyous recognition.
But we. We do not touch
Or say much of yesterday and whatever hurt
Muffles this knowing. Yet. . .in glowing word to all
I speak of her accomplishment of this or that
And the fact she dines with the sainted members
    Of the presbytery.
But see . . . we've codified in heart
That from our start some things were quite horribly amiss
And neither ventures now to plant a kiss
    Of forgiveness.

THIS WINTER'S DAY

Fight!
Uncertain of your crossing . . .
Miles back there were the amen ways
And hallelujah days of folk
Tripping on before.
Now, standing at the door alone
Beg pardon - proffer nothing pleasant
Of the coming darkness.
Fight back!
Kick up all the fuss you want
Raise a commotion. Confound them of a notion
That yours should be a silent passage
Damn them who wish your exit speedy
Sparing them the noisome nuisance of death.
Let them know you protest!
Let them know you got better things to do
Than die this winter's day
      In February.

ANOINTING

You stand back scoping the territory
We thought of as our demilitarized zone
Our fear of your coming
Mitigated by the fact that none
Acknowledged your existence.

You stalk.
Patient. Unperturbed
By those who pray you've gone away
      Confounded.
And so you come   into this room
By this bed   anointing her head
      For sacrifice.

SHE LAY DYING

She lay dying
In a room of well wishers
With anointing oils to foil demons
And prayin mothers of the church of the Most High.
They would not let her speak her rage
      Or fear,
Nor hear her protestations.
But. . . even oiled down 'n prayed up
With abrupt incantations of "be healed, be healed"
Her life was sealed in sets of tubes runnin
      'n hummin -
Her closing lullaby.

ABOUT WASHINGTON

What I remember about Washington
Was growing up in a house on a corner on a street
Where every neighbor knew your name
And your grandma heard 'bout everything you did.
Motha was nobody's fool. She set down rules
On crossing streets and strangers to shun
And how to run from dirty old men in their cool Cadillac coupes.
She banned hoola-hoops, cards and dancin
Though we pranced a mean Birdland behind her back
Had a great white Shepherd named Sporty-Jack.
And, all of the folk that mattered were Black.

What I remember about Washington
Was the day my daddy died
And coming home for lunch from Parkview
And Motha telling us so, and me, wondering, "who?"
And how was I to grieve for a face I couldn't recall
And arms neva crawled too.
What I remember in that day when a funeral was a funeral
And not a going home celebration
Is my mama coming home in a Capitol Cab
Saying we was too young - - and he was too drunk
And neva done nothin for yo no how
And yo don't need him no way
And I remember feeling awful cold
'bout the cruel things the old folk would say.

What I remember about Washington - what I do recall
Was that I couldn't try on hats at Woodies in the fall
Or swim at Glen Echo in summer
And that I couldn't eat at the counter at McCrory's
    On 14th street
When I had a dollar for paper dolls.
And I remember walking the hill of Georgia to Petworth Library
Reading dick 'n Jane and history book and Bibles
Liable to lug them all home in the snow
But, finally coming to know -- I would neva read about me.

What I remember about Washington
Was that all the men at the Soldier's Home on Park Place
    were White
And the bitching bite of the little White lady mid-way our block
We said howdy to
And Larry - the Jew at the corner store
Motha sent me to for thick slice bologna on her account
And Daddy's "Red Line News" from the bottom of the stack.
But, still the folk that mattered to me were Black.

What I remember about Washington was Rehoboth
That old Greek-Orthodox facade
Where God was to dwell
And I would encounter life only in preparation for death
And, choice seating at the throne
And how I groaned and repented my eight-year old sin
Courting a spirit I could not win or satisfy.
What I remember about Washington-

Was that on the big March day in 63 - I was not there -
Because my bishop and my elders would righteously swear
That one of them was a trouble-maker and the other a liar
And "you's a saint now chile, you needs to come up higher."
So they sent a check and let us pray and weep
But, in the days of that thunder, I was fast asleep.
And when the storm had past, and I would raise my head
Medgar, Malcolm and Martin was dead.

What I remember about Washington
Was the coming of Resurrection City
And po' folk asking for pity in the mud on the mall
And the unheard call of Janey being gang-raped behind a tent
And the thirty years she spent with that wound and that pain
Seeking her virginity over and over and over again.
But, then I do remember Billy
Wiggling in his gym shorts on the ballfield of Ballou
And the blue hard feel of the boy who first loved me
Who, may mama said, was too Black . . . much too dark
"You gots ta watch out for your chil'ren, dear heart."

What I remember about Washington, is me,
      Being all of eighteen
And the friends I knew - disappearing. The girls
To government typing pools and babies
And the boys to Vietnamese battlefields
Some of them never returning
And those that did - never, ever being quite the same again.
And I remember looking for them sometimes

And Lord knows, needing them,
And often seeing them under M Street Bridge
Or Seventh-street corner-gatherings absent hope -
Their dope and gin - thinning the dreams
Of the dark-skin crew I knew from Douglas Dwellings.
And if there be some virtue to this telling. . .of me
Going through the motion of missionary and maidenhood
Marriage and motherhood
Missing the meaning
And making meaning where none existed.
And never really being sure - -
Of who I was
      Or where I was
           Or what I was.
And how sometimes it all feel so sad
It's just being glad there be no righteous judge
Or hallowed way you must remember . . .
      But. . .you must remember.

IN GEORGETOWN

It's the noon hour
So I walk the streets of Georgetown
By Washington Harbor
And survey places I can't afford to eat
Or at least tell myself so. Years ago
I would not have been invited to sit anyway
So this longing today for importance and substance
Is based on something never held.
But, the water is free.
The boats calling into port are mine.
Even not owning them they are mine to watch and dream of.
Though white men - boring into work-day harbor -
Bronzed skinned and burnt
Speak of power and the lazy ease of wealth -
My dreams are not of these - but the waterways
I've traveled alone without you, black prince,
Hoping you'd catch the lifebuoy
And we'd sail together owning tide and wave
And the beauty of the Potomac at the noon hour
      In Georgetown.

REHOBOTH

When I was a child
God did things his way. Beauty wrapped in trees
Birds, rain and bubbly lights at Christmas
Then. . .hangin' high his own
Oak soaked in blood and pain
Love and death drawn alike from one source
Speaking absolute ambivalence.
I tried to understand what love that was.
I tried to understand. . .and pat my hands
And stomp my feet at tarrying service on Sundays at 5pm.
But, I knew God should'a got it right the first time
Eden, apples, people and serpents
Together…in he said, she said, it said. . .
Sure for disaster.

'Cause I thought, in creating all. . .evil was expendable
And there was little need of menstrual cramps
Lying lovers and stones peltin prostitutes. . .and death.
But I figured I could call
And all would be well . . .
When I was a child.

When I was a child
I was always afraid - looking at cloud formations
Watching the sky for cracks
List'nin for strong sounding trumpets
    From the east. Contemplating fire.
I tried not being a liar
Takin Madelyn's eraser in first grade

And Daddy's Guldens's mustard
And little Henry rubbing my leg under the table
Was by no means consensual.
But God was always angry
And nothing I could do
Ever drew me close to him certainly . . .
When I was a child.

When I was a child
I'd hold myself in the night
Wishing someone were holding me
And, that it was not rape
God showing slight preference for rapist, of course.
Cause, I was rape-able, you understand - -
Fat, nappy-headed, virginal
And evidently knowing violation I didn't scream or resist
And when my mama walked into the house
I sealed my sin in stone
And washed blood and flushed it in a commode
And climbed beneath the covers - - shivering.
Then . . . I suppose . . . he made love to her . . . go figure_.
When I was a child . . .

When I was a child
Ed Sullivan was fine for Pearl Bailey and Nat Cole
But no soul motioned me to move from clips of the
Holocaust
And bodies lying rottin piled in pits
And smoke seeping from crematoriums.
And being small - - and God being big - -
And mean and responsible and awful
And full of love suffering little children to come
     I came . . .
And the places of my heart slammed silent.

Days floating on crystal air I am still there
Hiding behind chairs
Curling in comers - head under tent from couch to couch
Held by fastenings of teddy bears
And books strewn about.
You learn to shut things out
Your grandfather beating your uncle - - naked --
Somebody shaving your doll's head and saying it was you
You - standin in stairwells dress tom and hair undone
And cousin Jerome wrestling himself on top of you
With them all watching. with them ALL watching.
And not a one coming to rescue . . .
When I was a child.

When I was a child - - those days - -
    I didn't have a feeling God loved
Only waited for appropriate time and sin
So he could win
And do his God-thing - - casting me away.
And I suppose - - shoutin the aisles at Rehoboth was OK
Till Motha- Dickerson led you to the air
And the stare of folk outside on the corner on 8th and L
And all yow'. feelings of doom came back . . .
    Cold.
Now. being somewhat old
I remember that in my tent
I could forget Vampire Bats at Monroe School
And Bishop Michaux's devil.
At least for a while . . .
When I was child.

WHEN I DIE

When I die
And nothing much is spoken of me
Or remembered of me
Or held in ancestral pantheons
For ageless generativity
Not smell
Nor smile
Nor the smitten heart of the boy I kissed
In the hall
In the dark
On a stark day of a Southeast D. C. winter
Not the scent of his body on mine
My tears in the pit of his arm
Pleasant in pine and Old English
And the hit of tuneful Tempts
Talking 'bout "My Girl"
'n my mama's "pearls before swine" - was useless to my mind
Cause he was fine!

When I die
And it's evident such touch and youthful kisses
And the wishes of my life are relegated
To crimes and omissions
Commissions in thought and word
Thinking no one heard -
Except God's a voyeur
And all impassioned deeds
He heeds in an accounting

Mounting with indelible ink on stone
That the known cause of your calamity
Was life?
And the host will go on doing what they be doing
Loving. laughing. living
Leaving the thought of death
To the sick and the old

When I die
Some days hence
And old photos lying in drawers are faded
And unmarked
And you can't name the face or recall the time
Given all of your faculties
Or the prodding of remnant branches.

When I die
Who'll remember the cry
Of Olivia and Tave in a Branch Fork Church
Birches braided through tombstones
Testifying in Spotsylvania fields spotted with the whip
      And the chain
And Stubbs men mingling and mixing our harvest
With pale pedigree?

When I die
And like me, you don't visit graves
Or plant flowers
Or publish memorials in the Washington Post
Or light candles
Or set by an empty chair at celebration

Laying low libations' liquid
Dried on the lips of callous chance - -
Then. . .who will dance in ceremony with our fathers
Who will call the spirit of the four winds
      To our circle
Fire sticks whiffing our smoke to the temple of our progeny?
Who will remember Granny and Daddy
Helen and Teresa and Wesley and Elmo and Vy
Who will remember Mother Crawley, and Mother Hill,
Lllian ,Tom, Gladys, Julian, Winifred and William T.
Who will remember Evelyn . . .
Who will remember - that she - was my mother?

When I die
And all I've ever done
Lay fallowed by rule, regulation and rhetoric
And rigid righteousness and wrong
And soul songs are serrated and separated
Into sinking soil
Toppled by torrid tragedy
Tugging at what might have been.

When I die
Closer now than I have ever been
Tock and tick tipping
Tomorrow towards our oblivion or joy . . .
Who will be the griot of our purpose
Tell our story ages hence
Who will go into the holy of holies
Light the fire, stroke the flame,
So that our name will not forever vanish
      From The Book.

A WOMAN'S PARANOIA

ANALYSES

If a woman is sad
She is a poet

If a woman is angry
She is a bitch

If a woman is happy
She is a FOOL!

I AM . . .

The crazy Black Woman
Who jots down demi-ditties
      And lost you
On the way to finding me.

If I had known how lost I was
I would have gone another way
      To circumvent the pain
Of you not here.

SEEIN RED

Sometimes, lonely don't see red.
Instead it have a habit
O handin things to ya fine and dandy -
Makin it over 'n givin it back to ya
Better than it be.
Lonely have a way of mixin color
Yellow cautions changin to green go:
Slow yo'sef down honey
Money and fine looks ain't enough to change
These crooks of yo mind
      Into a prince
O the charmin kind.

THE SPRING of that FIRST LOVE

There was the Spring of that first love
He was virile and strong
And nothing could go wrong with that fantasy.
Me - I was a child of dreams and nothing unseemly
Was permitted past the glass enclosure of my heart.
I could tell you from the start - I knew only happy days
And fairy-dust glazed about the hearth
      'n heaven held us high
Heavin heavy with our play . . .
Oh - but don't life got a way
Of waking us, and of shaking us and breaking us
      To bits and pieces
Piece-milling us back again when nothing's really healed.

There was the summer of our crying
He - the warrior god - vying with the foe.
Me - dethroned 'n prone upon the altar of his majesty
Yes, me - wide-eyed - wondering where
And how the wind blew tragedy to the strong-hold
      Of a love no god opposed.
Well, Lord knows, I knows - life got a way
Of badgering us n' butchering us 'n teasing us
To the tip of our own madness
With any gladness whipped as a strip of penance.

There was the fall we tried again
And again and ever again
He held the lies
And lain between my thighs

There wasn't much to say but amen baby,
    Amen Baby,
        AMEN, BABYl
And maybe a gin and tonic for moronic folk
Who think a wink and sorry salves all sickness whole.
Cause dear, dear soul - life got a way
Of providence and consequence and recompense
For every ill
And in the still lonely hour
Only the power of God trods the watchtower
Of our death.

I had a feelin you'd say that
She be bereft of hope
She be a low, lonely lady
Sad sacked and sickly - -
She be a joy-breaker
And she makin us uneasy
Cause she ain't for boogie nights 'n flights to OZ
In gauze feathered pillows 'n billowy blue
Like Billie's blues crooned to tunes of our passion.
I had a feeling you'd want to know
Why she gots ta take it that way
Why can't she rise and shine
In quit that pinning on what be lost
In what it cost /or will to toss it from she.
Why can't she smile
    Or for a while shout the aisle of the sanctuary
Like Sistah Strobel struttin and buttin demons
Danc:in down the darkness till dey be spent.

Cause this be the winter of she discontent
All things bend back upon themselves:
Smells from her grandma's kitchen - - gone
Kickball in the alley - - gone
Coppertone boys - - prone in the grass at East Potomac - -
      Gone
And the song of praise lost in the haze
      Of slaughtered innocence.
She has burned every bridge
And every sacrilege be boasting its supremacy.
See - - life got a way
Of harassin us 'n passin us
'n blastin us into tiny old folk
With tiny old hearts holdin horrid memory
      'n sorrow
Too much to bare.
For you who care
Spring be trippin pass again this year - - I can't go there.
But, be you friend or be you foe
You should know…
It don't play favorites.

PARADIGM

I suppose it's more noble
That we never touched.
It was all the same passion
And maybe more for the dreams
      Upon midnight wakings full of your smells
'n tell-tale signs of you hovering by.
I was no child and you were not deity
But I lifted you up in Crayola-wonder
Doodling you as thunder and cloud
And the shroud for my dying apathy.
Had you but reached across that moment and whispered
Some word of yes - - I would have granted you anything.
      Anything!
For it was at your pleasure that the world whirled on its axis
And sun obeyed its east/west crossing
What loss was mine - - declined in the shadow of your face.
I will hold this space for you in the menagerie
Of things I count precious and above
You made of me a believer in things better that what was.
That we have never touched, and perhaps, never will
Is not spilled upon the altar of regret - -
Is no torment for a soul
Set upon a path of joy.
Maybe in real time you are but an apparition
      A blessed partition
Between me and perdition and the gulf of no return.
I have learned not to want you
But, loving you, even without your touch
Is an act of will that won't be stilled in this paradigm.

I am going forth leaving just your shell behind
Your gift of love I'll not return to sender
Nor rend it less than what it might have been or will.
I am accused and guilty in this daze of loving you
And in the still lonely hour
I will conjure up this power
    And go on.

ROCKIN' AND HUMMIN'

He would tell her she was beautiful
And she would say, "Baby, flesh and blood
Don't enter the Kingdom of God."
He would say that he loved her
And she'd reply - "I must love the Lord
With all my heart, mind and soul."
The apostasy was his wanting her
And she seeing need only as lust
As she crawled into the tomb of her 50th summer
Thinking - if I ask it - it will come
If I ask it - it will come. But never did nor would
For she had numbed herself against starlight
       And the dance.
She spoke of passion as incubus plying her immortality
His arms about her as sure pathways to perdition
To the hardness of him as he pressed close
She chanted - Get back demon, get back demon!
Get   Back   Demon!

For lack of loftier word
She was a sad sistah
Seeing body separate and serrated from soul
She sought in the Volume of the Book
The lover who would not/could not personify
Her need for touch.
She took to rockin and hummin
And he to knockin at looser gates for entry
The sentry to the door post of his heart
Tight against true intrusion.

He would tell her time was fleeting
And she'd say, "one day is as a thousand years."
He'd say to her I am yours if you let me
And she would say - - "Jesus be my husband - and Him only."
The apostasy was her dreams unfilled
Her arms curled about him reckless
And his - - him still loving her
As he chose to make love to, but not love another
Knowing flesh and blood will not enter there
Flesh and blood will not enter there -
He wallowed - walking wayward ways
      Of wilderness.
He spoke of passion as gift
Gazing toward her for safe harbor.
Her arms about him as grace - denied and deified in absence.
To the hardness of her heart as he pressed close
He chanted - save her, Jesus! Save Her, Jesus!
      SAVE HER   JESUS!

HER FACE IN GLASS

Her Face in glass
Is not ugly (as some have said)
Not best or worst - - she's okay at many angles
      With the sun - -
She's creamed coffee reminiscences of Euphrates,
Rain-dances, and her grandmother's Cherokee nobleness
And Ebony/Essence girls turn stroke of brush just so
To mimic the proud lines of her cheek.
Absent those assurances. . .
Would you love her anyway?
What if cacklin' street dudes
Ceased their "hey sexy-mama, what's happenin"
Or old men stopped staring with more memory
      Than means?
What if she were the bag lady - in DuPont
Playing pirouettes to private pianissimos
Trailing trash trinkets
Slave to street stench and sickness.
What if she bore no resemblance
To Eartha or Angela
Or, being none too slim
      None too young
           And none too pretty . . .
Could she come to you for touch?
Pass your inspection?
Would you love her - anyway?

LONELY

You gets lonely!
You try not to call it lonely
But, lonely sound only as lonely can.
Lonely feel lonely. Body sweat and heat
'n magic memory don't stop lonely
Lonely be coming from someplace etched in flesh
Where folk thought it don't matter. Lonely cut.
Stab rather. Gut stab and twist sword in wounds
Lonely say your name in whispers nobody hear
Repeat it over and Over and OVER till you sho they hear . . .
     They don't.
Lonely breathe down cleavage can't nobody see
And only my heart know
The way wind taunts nipples to rise to notice.
Lonely be ridin my ass sometime
Mine and every other body I pass
Pushin weekday work like it change things
Hopin' Saturday won't come without a lay
So Sunday can,
At least, call repentance in audience.
Lonely be a bitch!
Clawing it way
Jabbering
Refusin to move
'n won't shut up no matter what.
It ain't shy saying "fix it baby, fix it, fix me good"
And, it wake licking raw and mangled dreams
     It know - -
Nobody reach that pit. Nobody dare.

That cave is mine
And daily it earth sink deeper, Deeper, DEEPER
Till even God don't go -- though I make my bed in hell.
Well, lonely be hell. Hell and mouths gaping wide
With no sound to alarm tragedy.
No sound. But, lonely be talkin' trash.
Got its own soliloquy. F'n' Shakespeare soliloquy
Supposin' speak in' it out loud will draw the crowd
And somewhere in the melee - lonely stop.
It don't.
Lonely hurt.
You gets use to hurtin after 'while.
You neva gets use to lonely.

BLUE PRINTS

I will do nothing but remember you.
What is my need of new experience
No. . . damn tomorrow
I suffer much today without you here.
What do I need of pattern, plan or print
Bluing possibilities of the future.
You were here
Now all vestiges of you are gone.
Your clothes parcel-post to wherever it is you are
      And I am not.
The rotten rush of your cologne is spilled
And chills the places I ly lonely.
Your voice on answer call says,
"Sorry, I can't come to the phone right now"
But. . .If you leave. . .and you did . . .
Your name . . . and I did   .
I will get back to you   get back to you. . . get back to you . . .
Ha! Damn AT&T and all pathetic playthings
Of advertised and amplified absurdity
You won't come back . . . you won't come back . . .
      You won't.

A WOMAN'S PARANOIA

A woman's paranoia   is not paranoia.
At least its not thinkin somethin is
        When it ain't
But, a history of people leavin in the night
Hopin you sleep or your weep in's muffled
In pillows by Martha Stewart - Home or Ralph Lauren - Polo.

Paranoia's not goin to the mall
Watchin you grab your crotch
As the latest hootchie-mama makes her way
In stiletto and leather.
Or whether on any given Lord's day
You forbid touch till 12:01 a.m.
But, then with flip of digital
You click another flick of 'Debbie Does Her Do'
In VCR
Demandin duplicate doin.

Paranoia's not that you only do dollar movies
Cold Duck and Hotel Six.
But that you don't do windows,
Or birthdays
Sunsets
Or child-support.

It's not your admonitions
        Of how much more blessed it is for ME to give
Than receive

Or your hand to mouth veiling where you been
When I looked for you yesterday
But here you come today - stumblin
And mumblin somethin bout a man's gotta do -
Gotta do a man's stuff.

OH NO' my Brotha - -
A woman's paranoia   is knowin she know
        She know - these things be true
And neva findin the courage to say
"ENOUGH OF YO STUFF'"
And walk away - from you.

ONE WHO LOVES ME

One who loves me
Will walk within these walls
And see thoroughly desecrated self - and say to me -
"It don't matter baby - you be betta tomorrow"
He will hold my hand and heart
Not parting them asunder with shadow
He will hear my woman's wail 'n show her tales
Of chivalrous knights - not frighten of his own annihilation
He will give oblation to my loving. Loving rivers
He will whisper by the water everlasting covenant
Bent to ebb and flow
And he will know no no. . .to tenderness.

One who loves me will honor my mystery
And not say she is hellion
Or heretic
In the thick of love, his body to my body
His soul to my soul -
All old, old hurt we'll burn in effigy
He will question God, as I do
And together, we will shake our fist
Insisting on reason.

In the season of decline
One who loves me will remember - I'm solid
And he will stretch himself upon my hardness
Even as I'm folded in his caress
Blessing the milk of memory.
One who loves me will see me as I am

Vein and blotch and notch in belt
From lovers who stayed for only a day or so
And played me for the fool I was and is . . .

For his will be the love that saves . . .
That from the grave
Raves in raucous revelry
For he be the one. . .Who loves me.

ITS TIME

It's time to change de bed sheets, sweets!
Sweet as you was - there be no way
To savor lovin from yesterday
And this play in mem'ry fields is pidd'lin' pay
For arms not wrapped about me now.
I gots to pull yo lotions from de cab'net
Parfumes and potions piss against de wall of my regret
I gots to gets me up and gets me outta here
To loose dat fear dat nothin good will ever come again.
I gots to lif de shade and let de light come in
Then . . . pull yo drawers from the dresser!
Yes sir! It's time. . .I goes 'bout begettin. . .
     What be good in me.
It's time. . .I goes bout forgettin. . .you
Don't ya see!

RISE

You must rise with the fade of moonlight
Never let sun know you hesitated long
In dusty sheets in a strange place.
Get up! Shake of the stench
Of a love you do not own
Don't let it be known you just wanted touch
And the taste of other flesh upon you.
Get up, I say!
Arise! Before morning cracks night-scape
And the only voice you hear
      Is regret.

UNDERSTANDING

Let me understand this.
You want - unconditional love
Validation of yo manly pursuits
Whether they be conducive to my sanity . . . or no.
You need multiple honeys
To cure yo sexual fever
Joy junkets on the beltway at 3 AM
To find yo'self
While I keeps the hearth warmed for yo Odysseus return.
And right now my Brotha'
You are anti-meat and anti-milk and, anti-money.
    Work - -
Being the antithesis to yo Karmic channelings.

You need yo space?
Well - have it fellah!
Do I need draw and circle
Dare you inside
Baby - Amtrak's number ain't unlisted
Will Metro-rail suffice.

You Say…Chile…Why
Why you sooooooo hard on Me?
Man's gotta do things HIS way.

Let me tell you something NEGRO. . .
I cost
…Soft soul sounds
Symphonies at Carter Baron

Saturday rain-walks by the C & 0
Doors opened on my approach
Empathy for MY struggle
I cost safety 'n I cost fidelity.
I gives as good as I gets
And most times . . . more.
And, I needs
A whole lots o' things, My Brotha. . .
But . . . NOT YOU

STRONG BLACK WOMAN

I want to speak of foolish things
The copper color of yo skin
Your hair roped through my fingers
Veins bulging blue-black
Through rippled arms about me.

Don't want no words for nothing mo' now
Don't want to speak of revolution
Or the way you speak and there is pain
Centuries old - calling
From Black places only Blackness can hear.

Don't want to fix it all - the way I do
Go before massa
Say, "he ain't nothing but a chile, suh"
Don't want to salve no heart
Don't want to bind no wounds.

I just want to lay
In the peace of you . . . and me
'n watch you breathe like life ain't nothin but a party.
I want to speak of foolish things
I want to not be dauntless
I want to be   anything . . .
But a STRONG BLACK. . . WOMAN!

VANITY

This morning
The tears are not about you
Other times were yours
Times of the bleeding rain through the night
As I have lain in your arms content
Knowing it was of moment
And you would go as all other comers.
Your absence - like death - is a surety
And inevitables are not tear-worthy.

This morning
The laughter isn't yours
But my inept attempt
To party at the wake of this ending.
What morbid thought encroaches on this revelry?
Is done away with quickly . . .

Your face . . .
       Is the face
              Of a clown!

VIRTUOUS WOMAN

I do what I should. At daybreak
Up with morning-prayer and supplication
For my moments rolled a bit longer
And my bed not my cooling board. Thank ya Lord.
Just before seven - my children pressed and bright
Alight from sleep unperturbed
And scuttle to the curb timely and adequately pumped
For challenged. And, then, I clean things.
All day long I clean things
Dishes, doors, and doilies starched and ironed
Stiff up the high-back chair
And place mats 2.3 centimeters from center table.
I am uniquely able.
Gathering my wits about me
I sit on the right side of sanctuary
To punctuate at appropriate intervals
The finer points of sermon
I pay tithes and offering
With a bit set aside for the pastor's aid and comfort
And then, robbing Peter for Paul
I still them all with my best mea-culpa.
I am not extravagant.
Don't ask for more than I need
Or want more than is acceptable
I do without so others can have.
I must confess - I make other people happy:
They discard. - I retrieve
They break - I repair
They destroy - I restore.

And what is more my man is known in the gates
Sitting among the brothas
As my hands work willingly
And I be beneficent benefactress of bends and contortions
And portions of soul
Holding house and hearth and heart
Hinged on the edge of madness.
I give no less than my best
And yes - - I do accommodate . . .
      Accommodate . . . ACCOMMODATE!
It's just of late -
I can't remember - why?

WILL YOU EVER KNOW MY SOUL?

Will you ever know my soul?
If not, will I trade body for the sake of touch
Knowing much the ache that once again, and ever again
You have stepped into this dark, chile.
But, I am a woman mild
And I am sick of absence and loss
Loss and death.
Enter into covenant with me:
Lay here in my arms between breast and thigh
And, my Brotha, lie, if you must
But, get me through this night.
Get me through this night shaking crust
And dust caked in heart and mind
And I, in kind, will be fantasy for you.
I will cook and clean and mend
And tend the garden of your life
And in the day of your strife, I will hover over.
I will speak your name in whisper
And then scream - you are the dream no other can be
And the song I sing will set our feet to dancing
And we will prance as dancers do, at will
But, still, will you ever know my soul?
My Brotha, I am growing old,
So if not now, then when, my friend.

WORTHY

It seems that I will always love;
Though never one.
Come fill this space and breathe
Sighs opening wishes of complete coupling:
I am not fooled nor do I play the fool for long
Long understanding that lonely as I came
I will go.
That you splice the darkness of moment.
Well . . . welcome . . . draw near . . . rest
And let us speak of things we fight as truth:
I love you now. but tomorrow isn't given yet.
Yet could I bind us is solemn treaty
Spare no word or act as sacrosanct
I'd open my soul
      Surely
As now you lay in the swell of my breast
Your hands in the wet places of my need
Kneading life into deadwood
Knowing touch ain't promise
Promising to forget that knowing --
But. I am silent.
Tomorrow in some other arms
Some other kiss upon your thigh
Another voice in midnight wishing flight
Hoping night-play soothes and motions memory silenced . . .
You'll be alien to that place I keep
Hoping some lone adventurer wise and strong
Would dare the wild winds wringing waters in this dry land
Hoping some faithful witness
Thought it worthy to love me . . .
And me alone.

SOAP OPERA DIVAS
(Heathrow Airport - April 1997)

Soap-opera divas
And pretty girls in tight leather-black
Are in fact, the only beneficiaries of love.
Old Ladies pushing grocery carts -
Bent over tightening garters on wool socks -
Have no need, I've been told, of holding in the night.
Why fight this sacrilege?
I, of the graying temple and wrinkled brow,
Woke early remembering how not long ago
It was I in passion's grip, dripping with need
And able to please - (like I don't know now how to take you
    In myself
And loose your need for running).
Cuming tricks my mama said
But . . . she is dead, and her magic brought her nothing
But tired old men seeking compassions
    And cures for impotence
From flesh forever vanquished.

RENEWAL

She sits watching morning break
Picking the braids from her hair
Wonder if, with this artifice gone,
They will still find her lovely.
Dreads, afros, cornrows fill her dreams,
But she awakes to blondes having more fun
Coiffured and comin at ya from Mademoiselle and Life.
She believed them for a while.
Then, looked into herself
Refused lye and pomades
'N got a sage rinse. Rinsing more than doubt
She walked out into new feeling -
Fear that only Rasta brothas would look
And she doesn't do weed
Though Reggae suits her fine.
Suited - she walks into their office
Her locks not yet set in place
She stares into their face seeing amazed surprise
She says with dauntless eyes
    "Don't even go there!"

CACKLIN WITH CICADA

I been shakin' off dis deadwood
I been walkin' by de river
I been whisperin' to de willow
I been dreamin' bout tomorrow
I been havin' strange illusions
But ain't got no mo' confusion
I been thinkin' 'bout you brotha
You was here last night.

I been thinkin' 'bout you brotha
Just of you and not no other
Even fatha, sistah, motha
It be best dey run for cover
Cause dis lovin' it ain't over
You was here last night.

I been cacklin' with cicada
I been break in' bread for barter
An yo' lovin's gettin' harder
Brotha you done pushed my starter
You was here last night.

You been losenin' up de bow-strings
Man, we makin' pretty music
And dis music - it ain't over
No, dis music sho ain't over
I been hearin' crazy songbirds
I been singin' Gaye and Gladys
I been singin' in the shower

I been singin' rock of ages
I been learnin' all dem pages
You was here last night.

Funny, I weren't much for music
Like Malinde singin' soulful
But I got dis music in me
Tune and time and timbre in me

Where was that you gonna send me
You was here last night.

See I gots to res dis weary
Gots to get some res for surely
He be walkin' big and burly
And he walkin' up the pathway
Baby, it ain't hardly noonday
But just have yo say.

Lets dis session come to order
Lets us get us down to business
Yes, I knows the pot be boilin'
And the taters need some oilin'
But lets keeps dis groove a goin'
It ain't jes dat pot be stewin'
You was here last night.

I been thinkin' 'bout you brotha
Just of you and not no other
There been others been here playin'
But, my Brotha, dey ain't stayin'

Does ya hear my proclamation
Hallelujah, Great salvation
I done had my revelation
I sho needed one my brotha
So I sings dis mantra over,
Yes, I sings dis mantra over,
I been thinkin' 'bout you brotha
You was here last night,
You was here last night,
You was here last night

BY ALL MEANS

By all means don't say it
By all means don't feel it
By all means don't show it or pass go
Or sow into senseless time some rebuttal for this absence.
We've got eternity - don't we?
We've got years to grow fat and sparse and wrinkled
Trickling tears into crevices of endings.
We've got time to toil for kingdom come
- - Not ones to trespass piety --
We've got all this space to face God
With our empty slate of lovers
As if, among other things, God damns touch
As much as He damns holocaust.

Tell me, what would be the cost
Of you coming to me in the midnight press
When the best we can be, each to the other,
Is another body by?
What would it take from me - - finding you - -
Not asking for always
Not asking for salvation
Not asking that you pour your soul into mine --
But. only that you climb upon me
And into me
And speak of joy again?

By all means don't take me in your arms
Loosing, for one moment, your sense of wrong
Letting the song propel us past this ache.

In the desolate hour - - call me.
In the desperate hour - - call me.
I am not God and I don't hoard records
I am not God and I don't account it reprobate
That you state in the heat of your hunger . . .
    I need.

I am not God and I don't preach parables
    Or prattle peculiar tongue
For what I know is true:
You may not want to love met
But - by all means . . .do!

I HAVE CRAWLED INTO THAT SPACE

I have crawled into that space under your breast
And made a nesting
Resting self from shadow
Caressing inward hope
That this be longevity's love lasting millennia moments
Into the twilight.
Nights a hard place to be lonely; even heaven's
Too, too hot to handle not knowing
Who you gonna sit there with.
And as I sift through photograph and rotogravure
You're the face I see
      You're the touch I remember
            You're the body - who - way back in the day
I could wrap my legs about shouting Hosannas
And Hallelujahs - and do, my brotha,
Do those things you do with your lips
If I'm not remiss in asking.

I have witnessed the dying of love
Under the canopy of winter -
Leaves dying in the yard
As hard, hard earth lay unbent
By nourishing waters flowing
Into places to wash and whisk our seed alive again.
My friend, I haw reached for you and only saw your shadow
I have looked for your caress on many a haunted street
In the heat of an empty midnight.
You're the sight I needed most
      You're the body heavy on me

The limbs I've laid upon - that - way back in the day
I could play my play about - shouting hip, hip hooray
And 'Howdy-Dowdy' - and do, my brotha,
Do those things you do with the tips of your tongue
Thought I'm not one for the telling.

I have inched myself along
Happy to make your song my song
Tapping with your drum
Making each beat meet repeating beat
Knowing the wrong of borrowing another's solo.
Hey, but, slowly, 0, so slowly
I have walked long miles thinking
To lie with you this spring
Sprinkling the waters with the berries
Bringing your smell into this chamber.
I have taken what I can of deadness
I have taken what I can of absence
I have taken what I can of silence.
You're the breath I've missed
     You're mouth I've kissed
     You're the arms - that - way back in the day
I could fold myself about shouting Ho - oooo
O…o…Go! My brotha, go
And do those things you do with your hot hand
And understand! 0! Understand my Brotha,
     I am asking.

EPILOGUE

I AM A WOMAN GROWING OLDER

I AM A WOMAN GROWING OLDER

I am a woman growing older . . .
The things I thought right fall apart
And crystal-clear decisions did have alternatives
Now searing "what-if's" questions on my soul
And I keep trying to awake from pipe-dreams
To cast of shadows of illusion - to see reality.
Cause when I felt old ideals sickening and gasp
I called upon my sure-fire balm
(I had cure-alls for every ill, you know)
But. . . hey died anyway. They died anyway!

I am a woman growing older . . .
I wander between wanting
To curl in the hollow of your arms and cry like a child
Or go out and conquer demons
I have the capacity and the need for both.

I am a woman growing older. . .
And righteous love don't come easy
But, is called forth and cajoled
From groanings of just what ought to be. So, I hurt
Where no one ever said there should be pain
And this "I'm OK" mask is etching sadness contours
On a face weary with perfecting
That which just can't be.

I am a woman growing older…and finding self
Means breaking with the carnage of the past
And no thing circumvents the pain – I've tried

(Its dissipation comes with time and care).
So…I have learned
That I can lose, and still stand steady
That I can hurt, and not break apart
That I can understand
And then forgive…
  And grow!

ALL THE GLORY BELONGS TO GOD!

ABOUT THE AUTHOR

Billye Okera

Billye Okera is a folk-performance poet. She was born in 1950, Washington D. C., and has been writing since the age of 17. Her work has appeared in Mynd Magazine and Dialogue, and she has performed locally at Cafe Myth.Com, The Lincoln Theater, The Potters House, Sankofa Books for Hale Gerima, The Black Family Reunion, Los Amigos, Barnes and Nobles, Market 5 Gallery, Mariposa, the 1997 Women Writers Conference at University of the District of Columbia for J. California Cooper, with Sonja Sanchez at the 7th Annual Martin Luther King Extravaganza in Washington, D. C., and with Nikki Giovanni at the Museum of African-American History in Norfolk, Virginia. Okera has performed nationally at Groove in NYC, and internationally at the Brixton Theater in London, England. She is a founding member of the Washington D. C. poetry troupe Collective Voices and performed fifteen years with them through the Washington Metropolitan area.

In 2001, Okera was named a Nation's Capital Poet in Progress by Delores Kendrick, Poet Laureate of Washington, D. C. Her chosen name, Okera, is Yoruba for "In the likeness of God: Poetry is her ministry and she uses it to speak to women of the reality of their lives – full of heartache and pain, but also full of God inspired joy and celebration. Join her for this journey to "THE MOURNERS' BENCH and Other Stations of Weeping and Joy."

www.ingramcontent.com/pod-product-compliance
Lightning Source LLC
LaVergne TN
LVHW051837080426
835512LV00018B/2928